DETOUR

Visit our web site at
WWW.ALBAHOUSE.ORG

or call 1-800-343-2522 (ALBA)
and request current catalog

Detour

*Forced onto a new road when our
unmarried daughter became pregnant*

DONNA COLWELL ROSSER

ALBA·HOUSE   NEW·YORK

SOCIETY OF ST. PAUL, 2187 VICTORY BLVD., STATEN ISLAND, NEW YORK 10314

ST PAULS

Scripture quotations are from the New Revised Standard Version of
the Bible copyright © 1989, by the Division of Christian Education
of the National Council of the Churches of Christ
in the United States of America. Used by permission.

Library of Congress Cataloging-in-Publication Data

Rosser, Donna Colwell.
    Detour: forced onto a new road when our unmarried daughter became
pregnant / Donna Colwell Rosser.
        p. cm.
    ISBN 0-8189-0911-0 (alk. paper)
    1. Rosser, Donna Colwell—Diaries. 2. Spiritual biography. 3. Mothers and
daughters—Religious aspects—Christianity. 4. Unmarried mothers.   I. Title.

    BX4705.R72523 2002
    261.8'358743—dc21

                                                          2001045905

Produced and designed in the United States of America by the
Fathers and Brothers of the Society of St. Paul,
2187 Victory Boulevard, Staten Island, New York 10314-6603,
as part of their communications apostolate.

ISBN: 0-8189-0911-0

Printing Information:

Current Printing - first digit   1   2   3   4   5   6   7   8   9   10

Year of Current Printing - first year shown

2002   2003   2004   2005   2006   2007   2008   2009   2010

DETOUR

Do you not know that your body
is a temple of the Holy Spirit within you,
which you have from God,
and that you are not your own?
For you were bought with a price;
therefore glorify God in your body.

1 Corinthians 6:19-20

Upended Universe

I have a strong suspicion that an unmarried daughter's telling you that she's pregnant is one of those occasions that burns itself into your brain. It's been ten months since I was so branded, and I can recall it as clearly as if it were happening now, which I'm glad it is not. It was January 7th. My only daughter, college sophomore, Stephanie, had been feeling "under the weather" for a few weeks, and had been to the doctor. He, then, sent her for blood work, which had been done a few days earlier.

The phone rang, and I waited for the answering machine to screen the call, as is my custom. It was the nurse from our doctor's office, for Stephanie. I figured I'd hear the outcome of the blood tests in a few minutes, so I didn't hang around to see her take the call. A short time later, when I realized she was no longer on the phone, but had also not told me the results, I called out her name. She answered from upstairs, so I went to the bottom of the steps and asked the fateful question to which I wished I'd never heard the answer...

"So, what'd the doctor have to say?"

I don't recall a pause, although I think a very dramatic one is required, here. She said, "I'm pregnant, Mom." My reply was the obligatory, "What?" She repeated her revelation, sitting in the hallway at the top of the stairs, with her arms around her knees as she held them to her chest.... "I'm pregnant, Mom, and" (with a little rocking motion) "I won't be able to give up the baby for adoption."

If you count like I do, that was two blows right to the solar plexus. While all the air was knocked out of me, I had the opportunity to consider that our family, now, had big trouble that I didn't know how to handle (and didn't *want* to handle, for that matter), and we would have a baby living here in... "When did he say you were due?" "Seven or eight months."

There are a lot of ways to respond to a kid with whom you don't get along very well, when they tell you they've just up-ended your universe. I'd even imagined (from a great, it-couldn't-really-happen-to-me distance) how I would handle it so calmly and with great love and acceptance in my heart. What I actually said was, "Well, con-*gra*-tu-la-tions! What are you gonna do *now*?"

There was fear and desperation in her voice when she cried, "I don't knooooooooow!" She hid her head between her knees.

I heard myself say, "Well, I don't know, either." It was probably the last coherent, logical thought I had for two months.

Hear my prayer O Lord;
let my cry come to you.
Do not hide your face from me
in the day of my distress.

PSALM 102:1-2

My Reactions

First, I got it straight with Steph that we did not need to make any decisions, right away. As far as I could see, we had months to work this thing out.

Next, I had to muddle through an entire evening without telling a single soul... without mentioning my despair, my hurt, my feelings of betrayal, my distress. This involved dealing with her four brothers when they got home from school, did homework, fooled around, and acted like kids. I had to make dinner. I felt I had to attend a belated Choir Christmas party at a choir-member's house (I said I could no longer think logically), where I sat in a near-stupor for awhile, and then dredged up enough enthusiasm for the goings-on that people stopped looking at me funny. When it seemed I would not appear discourteous to be doing so, I left. At home, my husband had a haunted look, and I knew she had told him. I slept out of sheer exhaustion, and woke completely distraught.

That morning, before my husband could go off to work, he had to witness my hysterical sobbing ("I can't go out of this room.... I just can't!!"), try to extricate me from the closet floor where I had thrown myself (he couldn't), and in short, watch me unravel completely. I did not see how I could ever get through the day. I could not even open the bedroom door, let alone the front door to the house. If I did, I would have to talk to people. I would have to be *normal*. I was used to being myself, that is, behaving naturally around others. What happened to me, I talked about with other people. No secrets. Now, my "self" was terror-stricken. And I had a terrible secret.

At some point, my husband, himself deeply-saddened, managed to convince me that I could get through the day. Mostly because I had to. Then he left for work.

That day, I managed to limp to Mass at Holy Trinity Church in Robinson Township, and when it was over, I found I could not leave. I couldn't go home and face Stephanie. I knew I couldn't talk without saying things that would be, *at the least*, unchristian. I stood at the literature stand, fingering the pamphlets, begging God to give me some help, and my friend, Mary Toward walked in the door. I sobbed out my sorrow, and we talked for a very long time. She was very supportive, and I kept asking her to repeat something she told me to say, if I felt I couldn't talk to my daughter. I finally asked her to write it down, because I was too emotionally distraught to remember what it was. She wrote on the back of a checkbook deposit ticket.…

Stephanie,

I'm disappointed, very upset and hurt. I can't talk, right now. That doesn't mean that I want you to leave, because I don't. I just need time before we sit down and talk about this.

Mary then urged me to call when I needed to talk to her, and she put her phone number on that deposit ticket, too. Then she got my permission to tell her cousin, Charmain (who had been through this a few years ago), and ask her to talk to me. She spent a lot of time with me that morning.

Still, when I got home this particular day, I felt relieved

that Stephanie slept on for a few more hours. By the time she woke up, I was able to be civil; a big improvement. I never had to show her the deposit slip with the short, sensible message I couldn't remember on my own.

To get through the day, then, took its place as the only goal I could hope to reach in my life. It often seemed insurmountable.

> *This is the sign to you from the Lord,*
> *that the Lord will do this thing that he has promised;*
> *"See, I will make the shadow*
> *cast by the declining sun on the dial of Ahaz*
> *turn back ten steps."*
> *So the sun turned back on the dial*
> *the ten steps by which it had declined.*
> ISAIAH 38:7-8

Life has taken a Decided Turn for the Worse

There aren't any words and,
    more than tears, the chest-heaving sobs
        speak my mind.
I can not escape,
    and my unappreciated life
        just won't end.

True friends hear my rant;
        watch me rave. They reach out... desperate
            to calm me.
But calm won't last
        I am desperate — to flee — to hide —
            to find peace!
Where *is* calm? I sleep and,
        unfortunately, wake again.
            Turn back time.
Heartache and heartbreak
        are unwanted bodyguards — so cruel.
            They dog
Each step and worse, each thought.
        I can't escape, and there's no place
            I'd rather *not* be...
                than here.

This "second day of my misery" was a Thursday. My son,
Timothy had a tap dancing lesson that evening, and I did as I
always do. I took something to read and something with which
to write. Doing so, I never feel as if I've wasted time while I
wait. This time I realized that a habit I'd developed as a teen-
ager might come in handy. Back then, at irregular but frequent
intervals, I'd just disappear to some secluded spot and write
what I called poetry. At some point I discovered that it helped
clear my mind. With my thoughts articulated I could come to
grips with them. Through the years, after I'd had children and
secluded spots became scarce or unreachable, I developed the
ability to become secluded wherever I might be. That included
these waiting rooms full of people and activity, not to mention
fully-functioning TV. I decided that if I had to live through this
nightmare, then I was going to write about it, too. I wondered
if it would help me come to grips with this, or if it would let
me down. I also wondered what my daughter would think if

she knew I was about to chronicle the effects that her very personal decision had on me. It reminded me of people, suddenly thrust into the limelight, who write memoirs about their difficult days, and then make money from them. I also wondered if my personal life-battle would metamorphose into something that could help someone, somewhere, someday. (Ridiculous! Look at what a mess I was!) Finally, I stopped considering my intentions. I just needed to write. So I did.

The living, the living, they thank you,
as I do this day;
fathers make known to children
your faithfulness.
Isaiah 38:19

For My Husband on Our Anniversary

John,

No flip, wry verse will do, this year;
No silly, funny doggerel, suffice.
I have found life so much a burden, this year,
And only your companionship makes it nice.

I apologize for waiting 'til you get home, each day,
To realize, not even you can make such pain go 'way.

It isn't your fault that such sadness exists.
Of all that will be ours, there will be long, lengthy lists.

But I do want to thank you, with all my broken heart,
For the wonderful way you do your best,
                        as have you, always… from the start.

Throughout January, I kept busy writing the birthday/anniversary cards for the family, for the year. I reached July 8th… what would be John's and my 21st wedding anniversary. I wasn't sure I should write that card just yet, but gave it a try. It is telling in one very important matter; I was waiting through each day for John to come home. When he did, "the problem" didn't disappear, and I would feel an instant depression. Every day! Thank goodness I wrote this poem. At last, I could finally stop expecting John to perform a miracle after work, every evening!

Terror

Can't make out what's up, what's down:
       turmoil's cold, damp, clinging shroud
Covers all I see and do.
       Turmoil's bilious, noxious cloud
Swirls through the body — free —
       to clot the stomach, heart, the mind.
Not undistracted by it;
       blind… to blessings God's afforded me.
How to appreciate them, now,
       I can not see.
There is perilous black
          Over all I do.
No savior, God, but You…
                and You say I'm free.

I'm sure a psychiatrist would have a word for this condition, but "terror" is good enough to describe it. At some point, a year or so after this experience, I realized I was "traumatized" by it — and that's not too strong a word. I was no longer entirely optimistic in my approach to life. I found myself "just waiting for the other shoe to fall," as they say. Although many people go through much worse (and who's to say I won't also someday?), this particular event blasted my life apart in a way nothing else ever had, and made me feel as if I were the dazed survivor of a cataclysm.

O Lord, why do you cast me off?
Why do you hide your face from me?
Wretched and close to death from my youth up,
I suffer your terrors; I am desperate.

PSALM 88:14-15

Diabetes

Now, another worry rears its ugly head
    (as though I hadn't already enough).
The year-long amorphous anxiety
    about death (itself, so breath-held tough),

Is forming inexorably into an horrific shape.
    I look on its heart-stopping aspect;
See the awful ways it might work its will,
    and I cringe at its effect.

Life is no longer an appealing surprise;
    not something new to look forward to each day;
No contentment, no peace, only dashed dreams.
    I watch the monster unfold its limbs,

And I scream and back away.

We made an appointment with my Obstetrician/Gyne-cologist, Dr. Denver, right away. He and Stephanie did not hit it off, and this did not surprise me. She seldom "clicked" with other people, and this was a particularly uncomfortable kind of circumstance. I think he was mad at her for hurting us, but I never knew. He ordered the usual tests, including the blood test for glucose level. He told us she could have a "light break-fast," but I don't think that included the large glass of cranberry juice she drank with it. Needless to say, her glucose level was high. She returned to the clinic for a three-hour glucose toler-ance test, and was referred to a Dr. Thomas at Allegheny Gen-eral Hospital.

This was all too much for me. I was already so busy, and now, in the wake of the original bad news, I was running all over the place for tests and doctors, and worrying about a life-long disorder that my daughter could die from.

(The death mentioned in the poem, refers to the convic-tion I had developed over the past year-and-a-half, that the police were going to call me in the middle of the night and ask me to identify "the body." It had dawned on me that Steph's lifestyle was dangerous, and I kept having visions of newspa-per headlines with a photo of the incompetent/abusive/dys-functional parents — us.)

For it is not the power of the things
by which people swear,
but the just penalty for those who sin,
that always pursues the transgression of the
unrighteous.
WISDOM OF SOLOMON 14:31

Ruined Expectations

My preconceived notions
(Oh—look at that pun!)
Of children and their raising;
of how I <u>wanted</u> to have done
Are slammed into "smithereens."
She never followed rules.
Would it have mattered, had I seen?
Would I have changed my tools?
Then I rue my method of raising.
I mourn the upright child
I thought I was nurturing.
She turned out to be wild;
One who takes the advice of others
no more knowledgeable than she.
She followed all the wrong paths
and chose living dangerously.
Look where it's gotten her—
though self-righteous—so often wrong....
A dead relationship, disease,
a babe where it doesn't belong.

A desperate fear assails me,
and tears and howling rise
Unbidden from this mother
with saddened, red-rimmed eyes.
I look at her, astonished
that she could be so dumb.
I wander, daily, shell-shocked,
agonizing, numb.
"The times have changed," she informs me.
(Who knows what desire fills her?)
But I want to get this juggernaut stopped
before it kills her.
Oh, Stephanie—you were, once, my little star
Look who's guiding you, now.
I'd give anything to go back and start over.
God! Show me how!!

On this particular day, I was feverishly cleaning for son, Timothy's, Confirmation party, which would take place after the service the next day. I don't know if a call from Stephanie or the doctor set me off, but I was sobbing and howling aloud, begging God to help me, when my Godmother, Aunt Bernice, called. She realized I'd been crying and said she was coming right over. When she arrived a short time later, my Mom was with her. I threw myself into my Mother's arms blubbering about how Stephanie had diabetes, and we sat down and I told them all about it. When I had settled down sufficiently, they observed that I had been cleaning and asked if I could use a little help. They gave me a lot of help. Lifesavers is what they are, that's all. Lifesavers! Thanks, God.

That led to this poem:

Magnanimous

I've never known such a faithfulness:
        sending help just when I need;
Looking after me constantly;
        hearing when I plead.
If human touch I desperately crave:
        someone shows up. What's more,
Each turns out to be perfectly suited
        to this unappealing chore
Of talking me through difficulty.
        It's miraculous, I say,
When I've gotten through another
        impossibly miserable day.
Dear God — thanks — I say it often,
        but it will never be enough.
You love me, guard me, guide me,
        especially when the going's rough.

If you turn to him with all your heart and
with all your soul,
to do what is true before him,
then he will turn to you
and will no longer hide his face from you.
So now see what he has done for you;
acknowledge him at the top of your voice.
Bless the Lord of righteousness,
and exalt the King of the ages.
In the land of my exile I acknowledge him,
and show his power and majesty to a
nation of sinners:
Turn back, you sinners, and do what is right before him,
perhaps he may look with favor upon
you and show you mercy.
As for me, I exalt my God,
and my soul rejoices in the King of heaven.

Tobit 13:6-7

The Heavy Covering Lifted

All is not depression;
    great, gray, gloomy cloud
Descending unexpectedly;
    mean, unhealthy shroud.
Friendship lifts it out of the way
    for short or lengthy spans,
And I *almost* feel like normal.
    Its unpredictable plans
Do not involve letting me know
    when recovering will take place,
And I just keep on praying

15

for the grace
To recognize it, and to fight
the blackness when it looms.
Thank God for friendships! Save me
from depression's death and dooms.

I was talking about gray clouds and shrouds — again. I
couldn't look at it in a humorous light at the time though. I had
been wounded, grievously, and the depression was overarch-
ing in its effects. Luckily, I had people around me upon whom
I could depend to listen to me, daily. Just letting me talk was
the best gift anyone could give me, for months. Come to think
of it, it still is the best gift anyone can give me!

*May he hear your prayers and be
reconciled to you, and may he not forsake you
In time of evil.*
2 MACCABEES 1:5

My child, keep my words
and store up my commandments with you;
keep my commandments and live,
keep my teachings as the apple of your eye;
bind them on your fingers,
write them on the tablet of your heart.
Say to wisdom, "You are my sister,"
and call insight your intimate friend,
that they may keep you from the loose woman,
from the adulteress with her smooth words.
...For many are those she has laid low,
and numerous are her victims.

PROVERBS 7:1-5, 26

We're All Affected By Her Choices

In all of this, it isn't fair
    To four more children — fine —
To suffer, as I suffer
    This emotional turmoil of mine,

But I cannot protect them
    From the frustration and fears
That I am living, daily;
    from the way her error smears

A mound of muddy worry
    over parenting. And tears
Accompany innocuous acts
    otherwise let past. Each hears

That anxious note of voice,
      understanding not, the need
I suddenly have, to have *them* do well;
      to listen to all I say, and heed

It. I'm much more sensitive, now
      to poor example: radio, TV, friend.
I see the quality of the fence is poor,
      And I can't go back and mend.
My hands are tied…
      and all they know is that I'm cranky.

Every facet of my waking life (and I tried to sleep a lot because it was a relief to me) was affected by this new challenge. Of course, sleep was at a premium, because I had four boys to continue to raise while I battled my way through this emotional morass. However, I do remember waking up in the morning and realizing, as I opened my eyes, that… Darn it! I was still alive and had to face this all over again today! I knew I should be thankful, but I didn't feel thankful to be alive. I often wished I were dead, but knew that was the selfish, cowardly quitter's way out — and my Dad said never to be a quitter. I also knew it only created more, and bigger problems; it never solved them. So, I was exquisitely aware of picking up a huge burden every morning, and then getting out of bed with it. As my mother always said: "You do what you have to do." So I did. Terribly reluctantly.

Comfort, O comfort my people,
says your God.
Speak tenderly to Jerusalem,
and cry to her
that she has served her term,
that her penalty is paid,
that she has received from the Lord's hand
double for all her sins.

ISAIAH 40:1-2

Sick and Tired of It

This tale of woe is aging,
and I'm tired of its telling.

Instead of howls and cries of pain;
just quiet tears upwelling.

I can laugh, albeit ruefully,
when I speak of it to a friend,

But it takes no heavy push
to bring the humor to an end.

Frustration, for the present,
focuses on decisions, yet, unmade,

And how I tail along behind
the "captain" of this parade.

It's the last thing that I wanted;
no 'aye' vote did I cast.

Yet, here I am — here, all of us —
just trying to hold on fast;

Desperate for a glimpse of some
unselfish 'mother' thought;

Hoping she will think first of the baby
and the chances it has got

To have a happy home:
two adoring parents near.

Instead, "I'll name him this or that.
What do you think, Mother, dear?"

I'll probably manage — barely —
until more than feelings show.

How I'll handle that,
I just don't know.

I *do* know I'll go crazy…
I'll go mad, without a doubt…

If she doesn't get a full-time job
when this semester's out.

Just getting through the day
has never seemed so hard or drear.

It can only get *more* difficult
as that due date draws more near.

It had been two months, by now, that I was living this
nightmare, and I was getting tired of it as a topic of conversation. Not that I spoke of it to everyone. I just assumed that everyone would eventually know, and sometimes the desire to
just have the announcement made and not have to think about
the reactions of others or myself would be very strong. However, I also felt as if I were announcing my daughter's sins,

which felt wrong and scandalous. So, I told whom I told according to circumstances. Circumstances were such that I, surprisingly, never told any member of the choir (with whom I practiced, weekly, for two hours, and with whom I sang at Mass each Sunday for the same length of time!) until much later. Because of this method of imparting news, it's clear, in hindsight, that, had we been conducting a "what if" session, and I were to choose those with whom I'd be most likely to share information of a personal nature, I would have been a bit wide of the beam. This was a revealing situation, in many ways.

I also discovered that, probably because talking about the situation was so emotionally-draining, I actually came to appreciate that I had places I could go and interact with people who didn't know about it and, therefore, wouldn't talk about it. It was only now that I could appreciate that, though. Early on, I felt nearly combustible when I was sitting among all those friends, unable to share my bad news with them.

I had many needs. I thank God they were met.

Even the sparrow finds a home,
and the swallow a nest for herself,
where she may lay her young,
at your altars, O Lord of hosts,
my King and my God.
Happy are those who live in your house,
ever singing your praise.

PSALM 84:3-4

And now, my children, listen to me:
happy are those who keep my ways.
Hear instruction and be wise,
and do not neglect it.
Happy is the one who listens to me,
watching daily at my gates,
waiting beside my doors.
For whoever finds me finds life
and obtains favor from the Lord;
but those who miss me injure themselves;
all who hate me love death.

Proverbs 8:32-36

Self-Disrespect

What would I say to Stephanie,
    if she desired to hear my voice?
She already knows — it should be clear —
    she's made a sinful choice.
She's put a brand-new person
    in a pretty awful bind,
And to herself, I wouldn't say
    she's been too awfully kind.
I'd say, "What can your opinion be
    of yourself, if you treat yourself this way?
Why can't you be patient?
    Wait for the man God picks," I'd say.
And, as for your decision, now,
    I really see no good approach.
You cannot support a family...
    Adoption, I would broach.

Lest you think it easy
　　to say these simple things,
Imagine an adoption
　　and the sorrow that it brings.
But don't imagine adoption,
　　and the choices fairly stare.
What kind of time do you have to mother?
　　How maturely can you care?
How, without visible means of support,
　　can you continue attending school,
And hold a full time job, AND mother?
　　What chance have you with a burn-you-out goal?

Watching Stephanie these past couple of years, I began to realize that she had no self-respect. I used to worry that she'd run into people who were bad influences on her. Now, I knew her for the bad influence she was. I was afraid to have her get in touch with a grade-school friend, because of the things she would reveal and worry over how that would affect her friend. I also didn't want her friend to tell her mother, who would then have every right to wonder what was "wrong with those Rossers." I had selfish motives for many things, which I don't mind saying, and I knew, to a fuller extent, now, the pride in family I'd tried to hang onto through all Stephanie's ADD (Attention Deficit Disorder) years. Pride seemed completely crushed, as was my spirit. I hadn't mentioned Stephanie's ADD before, had I? Long story, but it led directly to the problem we were having, now. She couldn't learn from anyone else's experience, and even told me, point-blank and many times, "I have to make my own mistakes." My disagreeing vehemently had no positive effect.

Blessed are those who mourn
for they will be comforted.

MATTHEW 5:4

Facing the Sonogram

Dashed dreams — shattered hopes…
I look upon the sonogram
and it tears my heart out.
A few years — a marriage —
And things would be different…
same little one, but my joyful shout
Would echo through time and eternity.
The good circumstances
have been stolen from me.

I am bereft.

I feel awful — not wanting my grandchild.
Fault… blame — none laid at his door.
But there is no choice.
Many things change at a baby's birth.
All the preparations
would be made without mirth.
Only grudgingly,
Would I open up my house, my arms;
No child of God deserves that.…

And my daughter
Would never learn from the consequences.

Her path of "clean-up-my-mistakes-please"
would be set.

I am a selfish soul.

The sonogram was a rude re-awakening. I was forced to see the reality of our situation. I remembered how I told my Mother of my first pregnancy (how I walked into her office at the Mellon Bank building, downtown, with my bright orange, positive pregnancy test card, and how she got tears and pride and worry in her eyes when she read it), and I felt cheated, once again. Any time Stephanie tried to sound upbeat about any aspect of this pregnancy, I just felt distraught, discouraged, or depressed. She seemed to want me to enjoy the sonogram pictures. It just made me ill to think that they existed! Also, I had been calling the baby, "him," since I had had to call it anything, and now, they assured us it was a girl. For some reason, I continued to call her "him" for months. Facing the reality of this pregnancy was the hardest thing I've ever had to do. And, yet, I could only hope the best for the little girl whose life had started at the end of November, last year.

For I am about to create new heavens
and a new earth;
the former things shall not be remembered
or come to mind.
They shall not labor in vain,
or bear children for calamity;
for they shall be offspring blessed by the Lord —
and their descendants as well.

ISAIAH 65:17, 23

Message to the Baby

Oh — little one,
my words to you are not so harsh.
You are what they mean when they say
God turns all things to good.
You are an innocent, and I shudder
when I think what the wrong decision
could do to you.
You could end up with no father,
or a very burnt-out mom.
You could be one of those
very sad children who get shunted
From household to household,
with very little rhyme… or reason.
I fear for you.
If I thought your only chance was for us
To take you, I'd do it.
But I don't think that.
I have five children, already,

and the first hasn't turned out so well,
as you can see.
Two parents,
desperate to have you,
Are what you deserve.
It's just too bad
That'll take you so far
from me.
I love you.

This poem pretty much says it all. Deep in my heart, I couldn't believe I would allow this baby to be put up for adoption. However, whenever I talked about it with John, he seemed pretty set. His response always rested on "How can Stephanie raise a child right now?" I always had to agree that he was right. When all the cards were laid out on the table to be seen, clearly, that was always the final conclusion. This child would not have a "family" unless she were adopted. Somehow, through counseling at Genesis House (a crisis pregnancy center), and talking with us, Stephanie came to see this, too. The two possibilities of Stephanie staying at home and raising the baby, or of us adopting it ourselves and raising it, were not feasible. We didn't get along well enough with Stephanie now. I could only imagine the impossible atmosphere around here if we chose either of those last two courses.

One Small Question

The hormones have all gone haywire,
and I'm depressed, again.
Even the Spring sunshine, gladdening most hearts,
can accomplish just a small lift of mine when
It holds its breath and powers up.
Can't get me past its knees.
And I'm forgetting useful stuff,
like where I'm going, if you please.
In fact, I'm looking pretty empty
just above the turtleneck,
And all the crying just conspires to harm
my sight. I look a wreck.
I feel as if I'm right back at
the beginning with this thing;
The sorrow, the frustration,
wanting to run away; to spring
Myself from out this trap of
terrorizing unknown.

This, too, shall pass?
I wonder.
How old, by then, will I have grown?

This latest "knock into the abyss" came about because we were talking to my mother (the baby's Great Grandmother) about the situation while visiting with them one Sunday night. She didn't like things any better than we did, but she asked, "HOW DO YOU GIVE A BABY AWAY?" The ultimate, $64,000 question.

My anguish, my anguish! I writhe in pain!
Oh, the walls of my heart!
My heart is beating wildly;
I cannot keep silent;
for I hear the sound of the trumpet,
the alarm of war.
Disaster overtakes disaster
the whole land is laid waste.
Suddenly my tents are destroyed,
my curtains in a moment.
How long must I see the standard
and hear the sound of the trumpet?
"For my people are foolish,
they do not know me;
they are stupid children,
they have no understanding.
They are skilled in doing evil,
but do not know how to do good."

JEREMIAH 4:19-22

Let Me Out!

A secondary nightmare harassing me,
from the moment this nightmare began,
Revolves around the possibility
that keeping this baby is in her plan.

I see an immature college kid
shrugging off the childcare yoke,
And continuing as if everything is the same…
depending entirely on her folk

For baby care and toddler-training.
I see me child-proofing — again — the house.
I'm again in the throes of the diapers
and "No's," and all the while, I hear her grouse

About how hard it is to go to school
and have homework and a job
And again, I feel the desperation I once felt
to turn the knob

and get away.

This is what I pictured, the first moment she told me the news of her pregnancy. My heart fell to my knees, and I imagined a baby in the house… it translated into one huge struggle. You see, I had spent a year or two deciding if I wanted to try to have one more child of my own, and had, only this past year, come to grips with the reality that I was through with childbearing; if I had anything to say about it! We used Natural Family Planning, and that always means that God has the last word, as long as we continue to make love. Chances were, we were done. I began to get used to a different stage of life… having all the kids in school. Until Stephanie started to act up, big time, I thought it fairly pleasant.

The words of the Teacher, the son of David, king in Jerusalem.
Vanity of vanities, says the Teacher,
vanity of vanities! All is vanity.
What do people gain from all the toil
at which they toil under the sun?
A generation goes, and a generation comes,
but the earth remains forever.
The sun rises and the sun goes down,
and hurries to the place where it rises.
The wind blows to the south,
and goes around to the north;
round and round goes the wind,
and on its circuits the wind returns.
All streams run to the sea, but the sea is not full;
to the place where the streams flow,
there they continue to flow.
All things are wearisome;
more than one can express;
the eye is not satisfied with seeing,
or the ear filled with hearing.
What has been is what will be,
and what has been done is what will be done;
there is nothing new under the sun.
Is there a thing of which it is said, "See, this is new"?
It has already been, in the ages before us.
The people of long ago are not remembered,
nor will there be any remembrance of people yet to come
by those who come after them.

ECCLESIASTES 1:1-11

Lies — or — Hanging in There

I've always felt so honest,
keeping little, I thought, back.
When I wrote a letter or I spoke
with a friend — amidst the chatter and the yak —

I would talk about our difficulties —
mention worry and woe.
I never felt the need to hide
our experiences… so…
It is strange; unsettling;
discomfiting, to say the least,
To carry around a secret
the size of this great beast.
It's not something that fits readily
in a conversation. When
A friend asks, "How is Stephanie?"
I become distressed, again.
I have found myself responding,
"I hate to answer that."
No one has, yet, insisted
we extend our little chat,
But I have found — at this point —
letting someone in on it
Brings the hurt back to the surface
and I would rather quit.
I would rather not face it.
I'd much rather just pretend,
And I am doing pretty well at that
for the moment. Time will bend
And I will need to do
a lot more talking, soon.
For now, I feel "the liar"
and I sing a deceitful tune:

I'm just fine.

Every day brought meetings with people that usually began with, "How are you?" "Rotten, thanks, and you?" I pretty

much quit saying, "Fine," unless I was caught by surprise. Then I would realize what I was saying and know that reflexes really do come before thought. I fell back on, "Hanging in there." Just hanging.

My days are past, my plans are broken off,
the desires of my heart.
JOB 17:11

Glimmer of Hope

I just cried, again,
but there's hope in my heart.
She is beginning to speak responsibly.
May it go on beyond the start!

Her decision about her schooling
seems, finally, to be sure,
And acknowledging unworkable circumstance
makes adoption the cure.

Though I feel a certain relief, I grieve
that all is less than ideal.
Yet, there's plenty of time for things
to change. The even keel,

I've learned, is an infrequent,
undependable situation — untrustworthy, too.
For now, there is some hope that "right" will be done.
Please, God, help this child with the difficult thing
she'll have to do.

And help us, too?

There were little glimmers of hope, now and again. Steph would sound like she had finally learned something and would sound reasonable when we talked about her situation. I hung onto these moments of hope with tenacity. They were not frequent, and they were surrounded by the lengthier, more frequent moments when she insisted she could raise this baby and still go to college; that, surely, if we just wanted to, we could solve this problem, and she could have her baby and raise it here… we *were* its grandparents after all. Have I mentioned the cornered feeling of desperation she gave me when she said this? I had a very immature daughter who had three years of schooling left, who didn't think before she decided to have sexual relations while unmarried, and now thought we should be thrilled that we were about to become grandparents, and that we could "kiss the boo-boo and make it all better." I could see years of dependency ahead of us, foisted on a girl who hated being dependent on us! She was very hard to live with, and now, because the unthinkable had happened… she might have to live with us a *very long time*.

I found it very strange to be in this paradoxical situation, too, where I was actually recommending that my grandchild be adopted. Whenever I'd played this scenario out in my mind (and I did, being pro-life, and wanting to consider the implications of decisions that would have to be made), I always saw me accepting the baby into our house. Reality taught me something quite different, and only John's belief that we would ultimately do the right thing kept me from insisting that we keep the baby here. Oh, the heaviness of this awful weight.

A Card from Charmain

Outside: This verse from Lamentations.
Inside: May each new morning remind you in a beautiful way that God still loves and cares for you.

She wrote…

Donna,

Just wanted to let you know I've been thinking and praying for you and your family. Wondering how things have been going on your journey and if you have been able to find appropriate Christian help and advice. The road home may be long and rocky but we have a "friend" who will stick closer than a brother. Praying this card has been encouragement from a sister in Christ and one who has been down this road.

Charmain (Mary's cousin)

Charmain was the cousin Mary told me about the morning of January 8th, which was the day after I'd gotten the "news" from Steph. I was in an awful fix that morning after Mass, crying and knowing I had to forgive Stephanie, and begging the Lord to send me help. And then Mary walked in. She did give me help, and then some. On February 4th, I went over to Mary's house, and her cousin Charmain came. Char talked about her experience with her own daughter, and how they had chosen adoption. She talked and talked and talked, and Mary's sister (and little daughter) came over, too. Mary had prepared a big, delicious lunch, and I ate a lot more than I usually do at lunch. I asked lots of questions, and got lots of support. It snowed the whole time I was there, and when we decided to leave (so I could be home when the kids got there at 3 PM, after school), the roads were pretty bad. I followed Charmain for quite a distance before I turned off for home. I believe she had a much longer way to travel. I wondered if she had any inkling what a magnificent help she'd been. I thank God for her, too. Just knowing a person had gone through this without losing their faith (on the contrary, it seemed an opportunity for her dependence on God to grow), was very relieving to me. I still had to face everything that had to be faced, but I was pretty sure I could survive now, somehow. I was also starting to see that God was closer to me, and more concerned about me, than I'd ever guessed. And I'd thought I already knew how to "throw myself at His feet" in prayer! God pays attention to desperation.

Then Peter came and said to him, "Lord, how many times can my
brother sin against me and I'll have to forgive him? Up to seven
times?" Jesus said to him, "I don't say to you up to seven times, but
instead up to seventy-seven times. Therefore, the Kingdom of Heaven
can be compared to a king who wanted to settle accounts with his
servants. When he began settling the accounts a debtor was brought to
him who owed ten thousand talents. Since the man was unable to repay
the debt the lord ordered him to be sold, along with his wife and
children and everything he had, and payment made. The servant fell
down, therefore, knelt before the king, and said, 'Be patient with me and
I'll pay you back everything!' Deeply moved, the lord of that servant
released him and forgave him the debt. But when that servant went out
he found one of his fellow servants who owed him a hundred denarii,
and he grabbed him and began choking him saying, 'Pay back what you
owe!' The fellow servant fell down and pleaded with him, saying, 'Be
patient with me and I'll pay you back!' But he wouldn't listen; instead,
he went and threw him into prison until he could pay back what was
owed. When his fellow servants saw what had happened they were
terribly distressed, and they went and told their lord everything that
had happened. Then the lord summoned the servant and said to him,
'You wicked servant! I forgave you all that debt when you pleaded with
me; shouldn't you have had mercy on your fellow servant, too,
as I had mercy on you?' And in his anger the lord handed him over to
the jailors until he could pay back all that was owed.
That is what my Heavenly Father will do to you, too,
unless each of you forgives your brother from your heart."

MATTHEW 18:23-25

Not

How am I going to not look at her?
She'll be home, for the summer, this week.
And she's starting to show (wouldn't that have been
    exciting?)
But, of nothing exciting, I speak.

I cannot bear to see the change.
No pretending will there be, anymore.
How on earth am I going to handle this?
I yearn for those "days of yore"

When life was still uncomplicated,
and I had not a clue
How difficult it could really get,
and what we'd have to go through.

I am tired of being so angry
and of, daily, trying to forgive,
And now, it's going to be even harder...
Oh, God — how? How am I going to live?

Sometimes, I think about how this trial of ours would look to someone else. Certainly, there are those who are facing death, dismemberment, disfigurement, etc. who would think I was overreacting, at the very least, and behaving melodramatically. At worst, I guess they'd think I simply don't know what's important, and that this isn't the big problem that I'm making it out to be. Well, I don't wish it on those people, either. I pray, heartily, that no one else I know will have to go through this. I hope they never know this particular pain. I hope their kids are wonderful, moral, and never give their parents a moment's grief. May all children grow good.

Personally, I never thought dealing with this situation would be a cake walk (in my uninformed days), since I've read enough to know that it "throws a wrench into the works" in a big way. But I didn't realize the enormity of its effect on every facet of daily life. I am furious. It's bad to be this angry for a long time. I am grieving: my daughter's innocence... my grandchild's joyous entrance into the family... the sweet, motherly way I'd have felt toward my daughter if things were "the way they were supposed to be." I am ambivalent. In a situation where I could have been full of unmitigated joy, I have been forced into a formless emotional mess. I want to be free with my friends and acquaintances; instead I'm reserved and hedging; avoiding the straight answer. I want to be happy, and instead, I feel as if she's stolen all my joy. I want to be proud of my family, and instead we have a scandal. How very much I expected of life... how very little I feel capable of ever getting. I am an impostor, right now, and I don't want to be. It isn't fair... to me, to John, to her brothers, to her baby. Look what she's done. Every moment of the day, I'm dealing with some piece of this unfortunate reality. God, please help her grow from it.

Then little children were being brought
to him in order that he might lay
his hands on them and pray.
The disciples spoke sternly to those
who brought them; but Jesus said,
"Let the little children come to me,
and do not stop them;
for it is to such as these that
the kingdom of heaven belongs."
And he laid his hands on them
and went on his way.

MATTHEW 19:13-15

To the Baby

Please, little baby, God make you okay.
I don't pray enough for you — as I would,
Were this a pleasant pregnancy
of married daughter, and all was good.

My friends would have known from the very start,
and I'd have asked them to pray.
I hope that God has spurred me
to tell enough people who'll remember you each day.

Dear little baby, it's not fair to either of us, right now;
You are just an innocent, and I, though not so,
Still, do not feel deserving
of this thoughtless trial and woe.

May you, little one, never feel unwanted.
May you grow in grace… with aplomb,
And may you, my dear, little grandchild, NEVER
do this painful thing… to *your* dear Mom.

Since my thoughts were so scattered, I was finding it hard to pray with any concentration. I would find myself just repeating, "Help me, help me, help me!" over and over. At this point, I began worrying that I should have been praying much more, and harder, for the baby, because I certainly would have been doing so had the baby been conceived in good circumstances. Thinking about the baby made me desire the best for her (and made me feel frustrated, again, that the family that should have been hers had been taken from her). But I also looked forward to the day when this little human would have to make her own difficult decisions. Dear God, please prevent all the children from making this error Stephanie has made.

And, yes, it did feel as if she had "done it to me." This is when Steph's many deficiencies began to gel in my mind. She'd always made me feel uncomfortable in front of her friends. They had a strange way of making this parent feel like an alien. It wasn't until Jeremy entered high school, that I found that a parent did not have to stand on the outside looking in. She could comfortably be included in high-schoolers' conversations, she could walk into the gym without wondering what the kids thought or feeling as if she "stuck out." Since Steph had gotten "old enough to know better," when it came to behavior, she still didn't know better, and managed to embarrass me, constantly. Her comments could make me feel worthless quicker than you could say, "Idiot," and she just didn't seem to know or care how to behave properly. Her antics made me want to melt. We knew a lot of her problems in the social sphere were due to her ADD (Attention Deficit Disorder), but they drove us to distraction, anyway. This just felt like another attempt by Stephanie to "do her own thing," no matter the cost or whom it might hurt. All of us.

The word of the Lord came to Zechariah saying:
Thus says the Lord of hosts:
"Render true judgments,
show kindness and mercy to one another;
do not oppress the widow, the orphan, the alien, or the poor;
and do not devise evil in your hearts against one another."
ZECHARIAH 7:8-10

My Letter to Charmain

Dear Charmain,

I am so glad you wrote. I've wanted to thank you for your (still very) helpful advice at Mary's that day, but I didn't have your address. She said she didn't have it either (a couple months ago).

Your card is much appreciated, too. The hard part begins now, Stephanie is coming home from college for the summer this very evening. Things are becoming more obvious, and the next few months are going to try me, sorely. I just hope I'll do (and say) what is right.

As to counseling, we ended up at Genesis House and she has found it very helpful. I'm not aware of her having gone in the last few weeks, but after all, it has been FINALS! Boy, I hope she kept her grades up. You know how bad I want to hang onto something positive and "normal."

I appreciate, most, your prayers on our behalf. We are much in your debt. It is for all the prayers that resulted that I'm glad I told certain friends. Soon, there will no longer be any secret to keep, and I just hope the prayer level goes up, because of it.

I pray for your family (Mother's Day includes your daughter, too — and mine, come to think of it) and for Mary's. She's really got her hands full right now. God help us all.

Meanwhile, Steph plans to work at Bruster's this summer. As to the school session starting this Fall, who knows if she'll have delivered by then? So we're just plowing along as if she'll start school as would have been "normal."

Thanks for your continued interest. If I wrote half of what I was thinking while writing to you, it would have come across as very melodramatic. But I know you know how I feel, so I don't have to say it all. Thanks, too, for that.

Love,
Donna

I've noticed, with great surprise, sometimes, that I'm human. I am not aware of thinking otherwise, but I have been completely shocked at times, when I thought I was handling a situation well, and then found out I was actually "affected" by it! Imagine that! Imagine, for instance, discovering I was anxious about singing alone in front of a group of people. If someone else had confided to me that they were nervous about such a thing, I'd have commiserated about it, agreeing that "anxious" was the only rational way to feel. Why then, would it surprise me when I react with anxiety to the same stimulus?

Well, if someone else were to tell me that their daughter was pregnant out of wedlock, I'd immediately expect someone was going to need a lot of emotional support, starting now. And yet, I consider my need for the same thing melodramatic. Go figure.

As rational about my extensive need for support as I thought I was, why was I, on some level, always so surprised that I needed help?

For everything there is a season,
and a time for every matter under heaven:
a time to be born, and a time to die;
a time to plant, and a time to pluck up what is planted;
a time to kill, and a time to heal;
a time to break down, and a time to build up;
a time to weep, and a time to laugh;
a time to mourn, and a time to dance;
a time to throw away stones,
and a time to gather stones together;
a time to embrace, and a time to refrain from embracing;
a time to seek, and a time to lose;
a time to keep, and a time to throw away;
a time to tear, and a time to sew;
a time to keep silence, and a time to speak;
a time to love, and a time to hate;
a time for war, and a time for peace.

ECCLESIASTES 3:1-8

Friend in Need

Puzzling… this Julian…
the body-decorated artist with the pleasant manner.
Why Stephanie — now?
Is he an answer to our prayer?
Certainly, he keeps her mind occupied, and that is good.
But I have all kinds
of questions galloping about in my mind…
Why doesn't her condition
Bother him? Is it that so many have this past, it's what
    he's used to?
Sad. Is he glad

to know she "does it"? Does he know she said she
    won't
do it again, until she's married?
Does he feel that
the pressure's off him 'til summer's end? What then?
Does he believe in chastity?
What will he require,
come October? What will he expect? For now, this
    Julian
seems almost miraculous.
I could never have imagined this for Stephanie — now.

Suddenly, Stephanie had a boyfriend in Butler. The phone costs and gasoline bills escalated madly. The poem asks many of the questions this relationship put in my mind. I just couldn't quite understand Julian.

One major hurdle that I mention above, is that Steph has decided that sex is for marriage. This was not brought to light without my pulling it out of her. One night, after hinting on many other occasions that I hoped she would "learn something from this experience," I couldn't take the suspense anymore. "Are we going to have to go through this again in two years?" I asked her. "I've heard of that happening. Is it going to happen to you? If so, I'll just throw you out now, and get it over with!"

"Mom, I'm not that stupid," she told me, and proceeded to explain that she'd made a big mistake in not waiting until marriage. I looked at her, and decided to believe her... for my own sanity's sake.

Sandpaper

The only thing that works;
that makes it possible for us to coexist
in the same house —
Is that I stop being a mother —
stop guiding, advising, suggesting…
and be a stranger.
If I treat my daughter
like someone I just met, in whom I
have no proprietary interest,

We go a longer way
(hours, even) without a battle.
This is assuming
I do not correct
adolescent behavior or harbor
a strong opinion on anything.

It feels artificial,
and even, wrong — a person who came
from my body — an acquaintance!

But it never lasts long, anyway.
She requires such constant steering.
Even my politeness can't mask
That I have expectations of a twenty-year-old.

She is like sandpaper,
and I just keep rubbing up against her!

At this juncture, I can just about hear people criticizing me for not cutting the apron strings. I'm sure of this, because recent conversations have sometimes come around to the suggestion that a person can hang on too tightly or too long. This frustrates me no end! I have always considered it my duty to prepare my children for adulthood, and have believed myself anxious for them to grow up and get out on their own. My frustration stems, not from the fact that I'm reluctant to "let go," but because I can't. She's not letting me. (I may be reluctant, once my youngest are at this stage, but I'm certainly not, now.) I have raised one very determined daughter, who wants out! Unfortunately, her wanting out and her deep dependence on us coincide. On top of this, I (who dislike confrontation immensely) feel duty-bound to force myself to educate my kids even when they don't want to hear what I have to say (and I don't want to say it)! We are doomed to be adversaries, in her eyes, for now. And folks who want to believe this happened in our family because I am too controlling, can believe it if they want to. It changes nothing.

I loathe my life;
I will give free utterance to my complaint;
I will speak in the bitterness of my soul.
I will say to God, Do not condemn me;
let me know why you contend against me.
Does it seem good to you to oppress,
to despise the work of your hands
and favor the schemes of the wicked?
Do you have eyes of flesh?
Do you see as humans see?
Are your days like the days of mortals,
or your years like human years,
that you seek out my iniquity
and search for my sin,
although you know that I am not guilty,
and there is no one to deliver out of your hand?
Your hands fashioned and made me;
and now you turn and destroy me.
Remember that you fashioned me like clay;
and will you turn me to dust again?

JOB 10:1-9

On the Edge

I became nearly physically ill
when she asked to go shopping on errand day.
There was no maternity section in the store,
and we swept the racks looking
for something that'd be okay
To wear to church. "Nothing fits,"

she told me, and I saw
it's true — but I didn't want to admit this… at all!

I wished I could leave,
or at least sit, and be invisible.
The clerk helped her
While my misery stayed secret.

Sometimes, it looks as though
I've got this whole thing wrapped up and handled.
No problem.
But I am so close to little pieces,
I have to wonder
why it is she can not tell?

I greatly dislike shopping. I once complained to John that I go into some kind of ozone when I shop (speaking of grocery shopping, which I dislike the most). It's either a case of concentrating too fully, and being distracted if I meet someone I know, or I just can't focus enough when there is such a superabundance of items to pick through. Whatever, my discomfort with shopping continues when it comes to clothing, because I've never been easy to fit. Whether for shoes or clothes, I am just as likely as not, to come home with something I won't like or want to wear, because it doesn't fit well, look nice or feel good. Well, apply this deep-seated discomfort to shopping for maternity clothes for my unmarried daughter. I stood in TJ Maxx and felt ready to vomit. I also felt robbed (this could have been a joyful outing) and angry (I had to battle this emotion constantly). We managed to buy a few things, but I determined I would not go on another outing like this one, if I could help it.

I do not know if Steph ever guessed what this afternoon did for me. I realized how close to the edge I truly was. I may have been fooling a lot of people, but I truly was "just hanging on." I felt as if I could fall into little, tiny pieces on the floor at the slightest touch.

Love is patient; love is kind;
love is not envious or boastful or arrogant
or rude. It does not insist on its own way;
it is not irritable or resentful;
it does not rejoice in wrongdoing,
but rejoices in the truth.
It bears all things, believes all things,
hopes all things, endures all things.

1 CORINTHIANS 13:4-7

A Letter from Charmain

Donna,

I'm sorry it's taken me a whole month to answer your letter. I'm usually a day late and a dollar short!

When I think about my daughter's last trimester of her pregnancy, I remember it as being the most difficult. I wondered if it was this way with you and your letter leads me to believe it is. When I would look at Colleen laughing on the telephone or having a good time, being smart with me and her belly visibly swollen with child, I would wonder... how could you? Didn't she have any idea what she had done to her life? To her family? How could you be smart with me when you should be crying and apologetic? Unfortunately, I understand a lot more, now, than I did then.

Her hurt and sorrow could not even be apparent to her because of age and experience. The reality hit after the birth of the baby and trying to stick to the decision of adoption. I watched her cry and hurt. I watched her try to heal for the next three years, and making the same mistakes... again. I would often try to explain my position with this analogy: it was like being at a railroad crossing and, from my point of view, I could see the train coming. When I told you about it, you would stay on the tracks and tell me, "I'm fine, don't worry." It was my job to watch the train hit you, and then to pick up the pieces to put you right back on the track, again, and start the process over.

I forgot how many times I have disappointed my God, and how many times He picks up the pieces to watch me make the same mistakes again. I am trying to do this for others, especially those in my family. It is not always easy. Wisdom from above is truly wise, but I'm not sure I am an example. How do you support a child emotionally, spiritually, financially, when your heart is breaking? Not to mention all the other things we, as women, must do to care: run a home, some work outside the home, and care for others in the home, as well. Not to mention marry someone who usually has no chance of really understanding because we are made differently. Because Steph is coming to the point in her pregnancy where decisions need to be made and followed through, and lived with, later, I am increasing my prayer for you and your family. The worst decision all of you can make right now, is no decision. Steph needs to make realistic plans for herself and her child. You and your husband need to decide what you are truly able to do that is in your and Steph's best interest. When Steph has the baby, emotions are going to come into play for her and you that are going to make a difficult situation even more difficult. Coming home from the hospital, even with or without a new baby is not going to be easy.

I'm sorry if I'm depressing you, but at this point in time, these are things that need to be thought about because if you are like me, there was no thinking at the time it happened... only pain and tears, but the beginning of healing. It was small treatment to the wounds, at first, but things do get better, Donna. There were times when I felt I carried the world on my shoulders, but with prayer and good friends, all things are possible.

I am not a good writer. I have 100 different things to tell you and do better at speaking. Please know I am praying fervently for you and am available, day or night, to listen. Don't keep things inside. What you are thinking are probably things I think of, too. Please call if you need to talk and if I'm not home, I will return your call. Will be on vacation June 6-13.

God Bless and Keep you,
Charmain

"Which of these three, do you think,
was a neighbor to the man who fell
into the hands of the robbers?"
He said, "The one who showed him mercy."
Jesus said to him, "Go and do likewise."

LUKE 10:36-37

Card from Charmain

front…
> God keep you in His care

left, inside…
> God is… the arm that protects,
> the help that assures,
> the wisdom that guides,
> the love that endures.

right, inside…
> May God,
> Who knows your every need
> and hears your every prayer,
> Watch over you and bless you
> With His gentle, loving care.

Donna,

Would like to hear from you and how you are doing.
Keeping you and your family in constant prayer. Your friend
in Christ,

Charmain

She answered him, "Be quiet yourself!
Stop trying to deceive me! My child has perished."
She would rush out every day and
watch the road her son had taken,
and would heed no one.
When the sun had set, she would go in
and mourn and weep all night long,
getting no sleep at all.

TOBIT 10:7

Belated Reply to Charmain

Dear Charmain,

I'm glad you sent the card, because I had actually begun to wonder if I'd already answered your last letter! I've read it at least three or four times already, and discussed some of it with my husband. I so much appreciate your thinking of (and praying for) us. I am amazed how quickly I can feel so bad sometimes. I go through the days smiling, and for some amount of time, forgetting the whole deal, or even able to ignore it. But I dislike being faced with it (so it's awfully hard being in the same room with Stephanie), and I still don't think she's making good choices and decisions.

One very excellent decision she has apparently made, is to put the baby up for adoption. If she knew how often I cried about that, she'd never stop pressuring me to let her keep the baby herself.

Life is such a mess of confusion. I've never been an easy one for making the least decision, let alone a big one like that. Thank heavens for your suggestion of a counselor. Steph seems to get along well with her, and I hope she will follow through with her when things get real miserable around the birth. Steph is signed up for Lamaze classes, and has asked a girlfriend to be her coach. Good luck to them. This leaves me feeling left out, but conversely, very grateful that I won't have to be there at that time.

I understand your "train tracks" analogy. It was the day after Stephanie discovered her pregnancy, that I stood in church wondering how I would ever forgive her, that I realized I'd been forgiven time after time. Now, God wanted me to do it. Or rather, He wanted to be able to do it… through me. It's not something you do just once, in a situation like this. Day after day, I have to manage it again. And if Steph knew, she would say something like… "Do you think I care what anyone thinks about this? I don't even want your forgiveness." It's hard for me to put into words, but I frequently think this could be a lot easier… it shouldn't bother me so much… it must just be my pride that makes this hurt and disturb me to this degree. But what can I do? This is how it is.

Stupid things bother me. I usually write a Spring letter to all the friends and relatives who write me a note in their Christmas card. I couldn't bring myself to do it this year. There are neighbors (friends) who must be watching Stephanie change, whom I still haven't been able to tell. I think I won't have to! I am a member of our church choir, and know some of the people pretty well. I never told a single one of them. It's not like they will never know. Steph goes to the same church! But I can't bring it up, because it makes me feel too bad to have to talk about it.

This doesn't mean I don't talk about it, because John and I discuss things from time to time, and plenty of friends were privy to the information, early on, when I was pretty much out of control. They will ask me how we are, and I can complain to my heart's content to them! Painful as it is, I still thank you for giving me this outlet, and for your advice.

We're barreling toward the unknown right now, and I pray a lot. May the whole situation eventually give glory to God, but it doesn't feel very glorious at the moment.

Meanwhile, my Mother has been diagnosed as possibly having had a stroke last week. She is suffering pain around her left eye, and is having double vision. My sister wants to get her a parrot (because of the patch she is wearing over her left eye), and I have called her my favorite pirate! However, we are very worried. When it rains, it pours. I am very soaked.

This reminds me that I am aware that everything seems, also, as you said, to be weighing on my shoulders. My sister-in-law said something about "getting through this all right," and I immediately thought she was talking about me! She had said "*Stephanie* will get through this all right." I'm not sure if she was trying to take the emphasis off my feelings, and putting it where it really belongs… on Stephanie's health and well-being, or if she was just trying to reassure me from worrying about Steph. I admit, I have worried very little about that. Very little unselfish thinking, but, thankfully, lots of praying. I'm glad God can see well past my selfishness.

Well, there's the whole muddled mess. It's taken me an hour to type this. I hope you won't mind receiving a fussy letter from a fretful mother! Thanks for listening, once again.

Love,
Donna

What Next?

Another little scare;
enough to keep me hopping,
And another trip to the doctor's
to quell the doubt.

She's fine, they say,
and I get choked up.
Relief looks like tears
squirting out.

I don't want this,
but reality says, "It's true,
Deal with it, lady."
And I do; day after day, only glad

Though I don't want this,
now it can also be seen;
I don't want this unwanted pregnancy, either,
to go bad.

"This" referred to the pregnancy. I believe this poem was
written when Stephanie had a false labor scare. It was just ab-

solutely too early to be delivering yet. So I didn't believe she was, and boy, am I glad she didn't. She complained about a lower abdominal ache, and I told her that if she felt she should call the doctor, she should call the doctor. I have to admit, I closed my eyes up to now to the possibility that the outcome of this pregnancy could be anything but normal. Enough had been enough, and I couldn't face anything else. I didn't want to face anything else.

But my sister, Kathy, and John's sister, Sharon, both had their babies prematurely. It was certainly possible. But it wasn't going to happen.

In spite of everything let us give thanks to the Lord our God,
who is putting us to the test as he did our ancestors.
Remember what he did with Abraham,
and how he tested Isaac,
and what happened to Jacob in Syrian Mesopotamia,
while he was tending the sheep of Laban,
his mother's brother.
For he has not tried us with fire, as he did them,
to search their hearts,
nor has he taken vengeance on us;
but the Lord scourges those who are close to him
in order to admonish them.

JUDITH 8:24-2 7

Praise is due to you, O God, in Zion;
and to you shall vows be performed,
O you who answer prayer!
To you all flesh shall come.
When deeds of iniquity overwhelm us
you forgive our transgressions.

PSALM 65:1-3

No Doubt About It

Up 'til now, there could have been doubt;
Others who'd catch sight of her could have been unsure,

But now, she's been to a funeral home
In a clingy dress that left nothing to the imagination. No cure

Now, for the gossip, begun. No way for me to know
Who knows. The monkey, out of his cage, is not tame.

How many OLSH folk were there? Were they shocked?
Did she get a sniff of the stink she's laid on our name?

I feel like the family in *Pride and Prejudice*. I'm ready
To swoon over the enormity of it all. I am about to drown

In a sea of desperate, conflicting emotion. Sweeping waves
Of misery beat me…

and I wish I could just tell everyone and get it over with…
Yet another thorny crown.

Sadly, several daughters of a coach at OLSH had cystic
fibrosis. One had died before I knew the coach and his wife.
Now, another had just died of the disease. We visited the fu-

neral home to express our condolences. The coach and his wife put a lot of time, energy and, probably, money into the children at that school. So, we were often running into them at activities. He often said, "It's all for the kids, right? It's all for the kids. And these are good kids." Also, as the soccer coach, when Steph was on the boys' soccer team as a freshman, we got to know him and his wife — the concession table operator — a little better than we might have, otherwise.

Here we were at a gathering where the line offering their sympathies extended around in a circle through four rooms and out the front door. Many, many kids from school and their parents and the teachers were there. Steph's secret was no longer a secret to anybody who took the time to look. Since I had been fearing, before her pregnancy, a call in the middle of the night from the police telling me my daughter had been killed — in any number of ways I found myself reacting as ambivalently to this experience as I do to all the others... the dead daughter could have been Stephanie and *we* could be in this terrible mourning... and the evil thought — if it *were* Stephanie, I could quit worrying about her! I almost envied the parents their good memories of their daughter. Of course, I realized that we still had time to mend our relationship and that *that* was a gift.

As to the secret's being out, I no longer knew if the person to whom I was speaking knew or not. I didn't mind people knowing for, in some ways, it made relating to them easier. I didn't have to stand there talking about something else, while wondering what they were thinking. Such a distraction!

Happy are those whom you choose
and bring near to live in your courts.
We shall be satisfied with the goodness of
your house, your holy temple.
By awesome deeds you answer us with deliverance,
O God of our salvations;
you are the hope of all the ends of the earth
and of the farthest seas.
By your strength you established the mountains;
you are girded with might.

PSALM 65:4-6

Holding Me Up

It's hard to think positively
when my daughter's on my mind,
And yet, I owe my God some thoughts
of a generously grateful kind.
We've clambered over mountains,
forded streams, my God and I.
He's covered all the bases.
He's held me when I'd cry.
So many mournful moments,
since January have passed,
And look! I'm still alive and kickin'.
So is she, and then, at last,
A little person will be born
(as much as I resist it),
And I pray "alive and kickin'"
will describe him from his first minute.
Thank you, Lord, for carrying me

this long, dark, unholy way.
May I show my gratitude now,
in this infrequent prayer I pray.

My frequent prayer is "Help me, help me, help me!"

As I reread these poems, I find myself thinking thoughts about me like "Why didn't I get used to this, sooner? Couldn't I have just made an effort and saved myself all this aggravation?" The answer is no. I felt the way I felt. I did put enormous effort into adjusting. Another enormous effort went into living daily with my daughter. Don't forget that all the regular activities had to be dealt with, and that the four boys did not stop being aggravating themselves when they felt it necessary, because they, too, were growing up. Hard as it is to believe, I was doing my best. Sad, but true.

And I did not like being the unsuccessful mother of a "gone wrong" daughter. Each new day, a word from my daughter, a word from someone else, or some change in circumstances brought a fresh punch to my solar plexus.

I mentioned it before, but I found it so difficult to tell people about this, because it felt as if I were making someone's confession public: Stephanie's.

Meanwhile, God was pulling humility out of *me* in this experience. I began seeing myself as the ineffective mother I was, and the bad example I'd been, etc. There was only one way to redeem past mistakes (and I'd made so very many), and that was to depend on God alone. He came through time after time after time. May no word or touch of mine that wasn't also of Jesus, ever come back to haunt our future.

Terrors are turned upon me;
my honor is pursued as by the wind,
and my prosperity has passed away like a cloud.
And now my soul is poured out within me;
days of affliction have taken hold of me.
The night racks my bones,
and the pain that gnaws me takes no rest.

JOB 30:15-17

Tasting Terror

Oh, God! I am terrorized.
She'll soon be giving birth.
What a miraculous joy!
What an occasion of mirth
This would have been, in another time;
Another circumstance; some other day.
I want it over with, now.
I want it to go away.
A nightmare of proportions,
Beyond what I've yet dreamed,
Is coming to its climax,
And my anxiety is teamed
With a sinking, sagging feeling
That life is all sorrow and woe.
How God'll get me through this,
I don't know.

I was not exaggerating. When I realized, probably every
other minute, that Stephanie was really going to have a baby,

and then have to give it to another couple to be brought up, I cowered. How were we going to get through this? Together with God. How hard would it be? Extremely. Charmain had told me that she had held her daughter while they both cried after leaving the hospital. I couldn't imagine leaving! Never far from my mind, too, was the fact that Stephanie would find a way to blame me for this. True though it was that it was all her fault, and true though it was that she was not in a position to begin her family, true though it was that she had made this decision, herself, it was also just as true that she would blame me. Yes, it was true that if we had agreed to take her and the baby in, it would not have to be adopted. Yes, it was true at the convoluted tail-end of this awful ordeal, it was — truly — my fault.

I thank my God every time I think of you,
constantly praying with joy
in every one of my prayers for all of you,
because of your sharing in the gospel
from the first day until now.

PHILIPPIANS 1:3-4

Meeting with Pat at Genesis House

I can't remember the exact day when I took Stephanie to Genesis House to meet a prospective adoptive parent for her baby. When we arrived, we found that the woman had spent a sleepless night worrying about this, and called to cancel the meeting that morning. She was afraid she'd get emotionally involved with us and the baby, and then Steph would decide to keep the baby, and all the stress would have been for naught. Too painful.

We were irked that we had come all the way there for no reason, but I always suspected that the counselor wanted us to come so that Steph could talk to her about this great disappointment. (She had to work herself up for such a meeting, too.)

Stephanie chose another family, headed by Pat and Jeff, who had a biological child, now age 16, with some kind of chronic health condition, and another adopted child, a son age 3. They hadn't been pushing for another adoption, but had let the counselor know that they were available, should a child be born who needed them.

We went back to Genesis House, on another day, and met Pat. She, the counselor and Steph talked for some time. I didn't really expect to meet her, but Stephanie came back and asked me to come and do so. After our hellos, Pat proffered a stack of family pictures. I got through about three before I started crying my eyes out. She talked reassuringly, nonstop. I couldn't say a word. Pat met Steph's criteria, and seemed a Godsend. I just wished we'd be able to do more than wait for photos from them. I pictured their attending a family party at my sister, Kathy's. I imagined them fitting right in. Our family increased, rather than decreased. Although this sort of relationship was part of an adoption my sister-in-law, Ellen, knew about, in our case it was just a dream.

When the turn came for Esther, daughter of Abihail,
the uncle of Mordecai who had adopted her as his own daughter,
to go in to the king, she asked for nothing except what Hegai,
the king's eunuch who had charge of the women, advised.
Esther was admired by all who saw her....
Now Esther had not revealed her kindred or her people,
as Mordecai had charged her;
for Esther obeyed Mordecai
just as when she was brought up by him.

ESTHER 2:15, 20

Attention Deficit Disorder

Will it get easier, I wonder,
when she takes her Ritalin, again?
I've almost completely forgotten
how effective it was when

This little pill woke up her brain
and gave her time to think
Before she spoke or acted.
We didn't have to shrink

At every meeting, or duck at every word.
We saw academic progress,
And friends were glad about it, when they heard
that it was so. I guess,

If memory serves me right,
we may, yet, see again
A blossoming; a springtime.
Oh, Lord, please tell me when!

This poem refers to the sea change that occurred in Stephanie's academic and social behavior when she began to take Ritalin at the beginning of her senior year at OLSH. All of a sudden, she was an A-and-B student. Up till then, there was a D on every high school report card. She'd bring that grade up, just to have another one go down. She was also very oppositional about absolutely every subject. There were so few conversations between us that didn't escalate into some sort of battle, that I can't remember their existence. Perhaps I exaggerate, but I did so little "right" in her eyes, and was so tired of being on my guard all the time, that it was a relief when she wasn't around. Boy, did this disappoint and discourage me! I had so much higher an expectation of my relationships with my children.

Steph's senior year included a 3.0 grade-point average, several boyfriends, driving a car (and if one of ours was sitting in the driveway, it was fair game... she always wanted to go somewhere), a Christmas formal and the prom, and friendships with Nicole and our nephew, George. This means she began drinking and smoking and staying out late. Although I never got the specifics, Stephanie once told me that she started getting into trouble in her senior year. I know, now, that Ritalin does not solve every problem that comes with ADD. She needed counseling, but I didn't know enough then to get it for her. Too bad she couldn't have just listened to counsel.

These days, Steph tells us that Ritalin does nothing good for her. What can I say? We muddle along.

From Every Side

The secret is a secret, no more.
　　　　The knowledge that choked me
Time and again,
　　　　and laid me out on the floor,
Is common knowledge.
　　　　My humiliation grows.
I myself am amazed at how it bothers me
　　　　that she shows.
Great blocks of people are privy now;
　　　　choir, neighbors. Today,
Our extended family
　　　　will see the display.
I'll try to swallow
　　　　that lumpy pride.
I'll deal with the reactions
　　　　as I can. Inside,
I expect to feel molten and sick.
　　　　I might carry home
Even more distress,
　　　　and that thick
Blanket of sorrow I've worn,
　　　　this very long while,

Will probably wrap tighter.
    Then, I'll file
Another moment of misery
    in time's roomy bin.
While I discover, again, how I'll "get through this,"
    I'll wonder how anyone can win
                    at life.

I was innocently making funnel cakes at the choir's booth at the church festival. Steph came over to tell me something, then left. Fellow choir-member, Nancy, turned to me and said, "Stephanie's looking good." I said, "Right." She took the sarcasm in my voice for an invitation, and followed that up with, "for the shape she's in." The choir party had been at her house at the end of July, and I had overheard her talking about her own daughter who had been pregnant in her time at the wrong time. I hadn't gotten involved in the conversation then, but I remembered it now. Nancy talked to me for a few more minutes, but I don't really know what she said. I just knew I no longer had the option of informing others. This was headlines.

A new problem linked to this was that I no longer knew who knew and who was innocent of the knowledge. So I didn't know who was asking me how I was, and who, instead, wanted to talk about this. Very difficult.

...when I am afraid,
I put my trust in you.
In God, whose word I praise,
in God I trust; I am not afraid;
what can flesh do to me?
You have kept count of my tossings;
put my tears in your bottle.
Are they not in your record?

PSALM 56:3-4, 8

Beggar Woman

Ask me a question... any question
having to do with the baby,
And my usual response is crying.
It's almost amazing... no matter what I do,
it can be interrupted
By the sighing.

I'm beginning to feel melodramatic
and too emotional... but can any reaction
To this circumstance be considered overdone?
Even though I've been blessed
with emotional support... you would think
I have none!

I thank the Lord for the help
He's sent. Often
I'm not even aware of it.
But (and, with me, there's always a but),
I still need *more* help... begging?
I'm not above it.

Here's a note I wrote with this poem… "From a hymn I cantored at a recent funeral… *'Shepherd me, oh, God, beyond my wants, beyond my fears, from death into life.'* I hope our solutions are 'life' solutions."

There was a point, somewhere in these last weeks, when my walking partner, Sandy, asked me if I thought I might need to talk to someone professionally. She thought this might be out of her league, and that a counselor would be more helpful to me than she was being. She'll never know how helpful it was just to be able to talk to her when I needed to. She also doesn't know how often I didn't say a thing because I knew it would be overdoing it with her. I tried to portion out the confidences so that any one person didn't have to deal with too much on this same subject (and maybe not want to talk to me, anymore… I've known people who've said they avoided someone because their problems were just too much and they couldn't listen to it, anymore). This would probably surprise her, because we talk so much about it. She'd think it impossible that I could have talked more. Not so.

I am especially glad I could talk things over with John. My new friend, Charmain, had had an unsupportive husband (to say the least), and she had to deal with this whole, heavy thing, herself. I was well-and-truly blessed, and still found it absurdly difficult.

...but a woman whose little daughter had an
unclean spirit immediately heard about him,
and she came and bowed down at his feet.
Now the woman was a Gentile, of Syrophoenician origin.
She begged him to cast the demon out of her daughter.
He said to her, "Let the children be fed first,
for it is not fair to take the children's food
and throw it to the dogs." But she answered him,
"Sir, even the dogs under the table eat
the children's crumbs." Then he said to her,
"For saying that, you may go —
the demon has left your daughter."
So she went home, found the child
lying on the bed, and the demon gone.

MARK 7:25-30

Constant Question

What a week! What worry.
I am mortally pained.
It looked as if Thursday would be the day,
Then they got the labor to fade.

Something-ol and Phenergan,
and Steph was out like a light.
A sonogram showed her baby's growth
was not quite right.

Now, high-risk, again,
(nothing with her is ever easy)
And I am always crying;
feeling unreal and queasy.

My dear Lord, will it ever end?

I must admit my fear;
This, indeed, may have an end,
to be replaced by worse, next year.

I realize… with all my prayers…
I have to put my trust in You.
You can see how poorly I do that.
What am I going to do?

I took Stephanie to her regular obstetrical appointment, and she came out to the car, where I was reading, and told me the doctor wanted me to come in! Dealing with this doctor (my gynecologist/obstetrician to whom I went for each of the boys), was the only instance, since Steph started college, where a person acted as if Steph were still a child of mine, instead of an independent, self-sufficient adult, already. (I've mentioned that Steph and he did not hit it off, either. I was never sure, but I often wondered if he were mad at her for giving her mother this trouble! And mad at me, probably, for not teaching *birth* control, since his office was full of samples of these pills. I wish I would have had some luck teaching *self*-control! Since natural family planning is what we use, I could have taught her that, but promiscuity has no interest in it.) Anyway, I was inexplicably displeased with having to assume motherly duties in this situation. I think it's because I had been forced out of them in everything else, and I resented having to cart my daughter all over the place and pay for all this and worry about her and the baby, when a simple, "No, I won't do that before marriage," would have saved us all this trouble.

My fear about "next year" was reasonable. This was just the most recent "mistake" Steph had made, and I'd already put in two full years of worrying, caring and praying. I was tired.

Goodbye Instead of Hello

More than I ever dreamed I'd live
has been lived these past two weeks…
Stopping premature labor;
3 sonograms at 3 different locations in only 5 days;
Transfer to a high-risk center, with the concomitant
plethora of doctor's appointments,
And, finally, an evening, almost surreal,
Watching Chevy Chase's *Vacation* on the hospital TV;
watching helicopters land at the trauma center;
watching as pregnancy became labor, once more.

I missed the 6 AM induction,
But the phone rang at 8 AM, and there I was,
listening to Kay, her labor coach and best friend,
telling me my granddaughter was here.

And she is here…
all 4 lb. 13 1/2 oz. of her; all 18 inches;
lots of dark hair (just like her Mom's, at birth);
so very quiet and complacent (as her Mom never was);

born on August 26th…
Karynna Joan… beautiful baby
over whom I've cried buckets;
whom I've held once, and kissed,
and to whom I have to say goodbye.…
I hope your life is happy.

Steph had had a sonogram done at Sewickley Hospital. Considering the results, her obstetrician felt the baby wasn't growing as quickly as she should have been. So we had to visit a diagnostic center near St. Clair Hospital. Their report coincided, so the doctor didn't want to handle Steph anymore. That meant we had to go back to Allegheny General Hospital's High Risk Pregnancy Center (where we'd gone when he thought she had diabetes, earlier in the pregnancy), where they did *another* sonogram — the third in five days! Whatta pain. I know, for sure, I never thought she was high risk. Even with twins, had never felt high risk. I suppose, now, I see that I was the ostrich with my head in the sand. They said the baby had intrauterine growth retardation, and would grow better *outside* her mother! This sounded foreign to me, and typical of a technological approach to a natural process. But Steph did spend time in smoky environments, and didn't eat a balanced diet. And there was a lot of stress in this pregnancy. So, we did what they told us to do. And then, I had a grandchild… and a child who was a mother.

Again I saw that under the sun the race is not
to the swift, nor the battle to the strong,
nor bread to the wise, nor riches
to the intelligent, nor favor to the skillful;
but time and chance happen to them all.
For no one can anticipate the time of disaster.
Like fish taken in a cruel net,
and like birds caught in a snare,
so mortals are snared at a time of calamity
when it suddenly falls upon them.

ECCLESIASTES 9:11-12

You Do What You *Have To* Do

I have cried hard in my life…
Especially in these past two years, I've felt the knife
of sorrow wound my heart, over and over, again.
I've felt the weight of what could have been…
of dashed dreams. I have never cried the way I cried
when I felt the agony inside
that my daughter had to suffer when,
not knowing if we'd see her again…
we drove away from her baby.
What a horrible ripping and tearing… I'd think
no human body could withstand it. We'd shrink
from the thought. But there was no hiding.
I howled with despair as I drove home, confiding…
in God alone. And anyone who saw the haunted,
hunted,
haggard pain flaunted
by eyes so swollen, bleary, red;

saw a face whose expression, clearly said,
"No solution." No solution, but to live with this
    horror:
a granddaughter, so rich in life, and my own life, so
    much poorer.

This sad time didn't have to be, but it was. Since the impetuous decision to join with a man without a binding commitment, we had been cast onto this track of sorrow. Now, the hard part had come. As if all the hard parts up to now were nothing! My daughter was discharged from the hospital before the baby was. Karynna was having trouble gaining weight, so she was to stay, but Steph was to go. They sent me down to the garage for my car and I drove around the hospital to the covered entrance/exit. There, the wheelchair let Stephanie off at my car, and she climbed in, took one look back whence she'd come and turned back to me with the most tortured face I could have imagined. I grabbed her, there in the other front seat, and held her while she sobbed. It still makes me cry to think of it. I don't know how I ever would have gotten the strength to start the car and drive out of there, if we hadn't been in a no-parking zone and taking up space someone else would have soon needed. Off we drove, balloons and flowers and all, back to the North Hills, where Steph would, within days, be going to classes (which had started the day before Karynna was born). She amazed people, going to school right out of the hospital. She also surprised me, by getting back to the hospital any way she could, until the baby was discharged. She even shamed the father into going — once. We went about three times, even taking John's Mom, once, but it was difficult — in a major way — to hold a baby you really couldn't bond with, because you'd never see her again. (That's why my mother didn't go, at all.) I daydreamed about just spending the day there. I also tried to see her once without Steph being there, but when I called the floor to see if I'd be allowed to visit (being Grandma, and all), they said we weren't allowed without "the parents."

My Mom always said, when the hard things came along, "You do what you have to do." A maxim worth living by, but it was never more important than on this particular day. No excuses.

*I consider that the sufferings of this present time
are not worth comparing with the glory about to be revealed to us.
For the creation waits with eager longing for the revealing of the
children of God; for the creation was subjected to futility,
not of its own will but by the will of the one who subjected it,
in hope that the creation itself will be set free
from its bondage to decay and will obtain
the freedom of the glory of the children of God.
We know that the whole creation has been groaning
in labor pains until now; and not only the creation,
but we ourselves, who have the first fruits of the Spirit,
groan inwardly while we wait for adoption,
the redemption of our bodies. For in hope we were saved.
Now hope that is seen is not hope. For who hopes
for what is seen? But if we hope for what we
do not see, we wait for it with patience.
Likewise the Spirit helps us in our weakness;
for we do not know how to pray as we ought,
but that very Spirit intercedes with sighs too deep for words.
And God, who searches the heart,
knows what is the mind of the Spirit,
because the Spirit intercedes for the saints
according to the will of God.
We know that all things work together
for good for those who love God,
who are called according to his purpose.*

ROMANS 8:18-28

The Good Part

Deed accomplished;
small child born;
Another soul to see the morn;
Another child to learn and play;

Another one to end a day
Safe in the arms of God, above;
Another person He will love… forever.

Dedicated to Karynna Joan Rosser, when she was 11 days old. Made into a card for Stephanie's 20th birthday, with three photos of the baby and two Scripture verses.

I found that card I'd made, recently, when I was looking at Stephanie's small silver-framed album of her baby's pictures. She had tucked it in the front of the album. Maybe it meant as much to her as I'd hoped it would. She really had done a beautiful and brave thing, especially in this mean, disrespectful world. She treasured the life of one little girl over the comfort and convenience of continuing life without her. In other words, she hadn't multiplied her errors. I feel proud of her.

But truly God has listened;
he has given heed to the words of my prayer.
Blessed be God, because he has not rejected my prayer
or removed his steadfast love from me.

PSALM 66:19-20

Grief

If birth is a joy,
that explains my feeling,
while she was in the hospital, healing;

Before the discharge, and its crying…
before baby's discharge, and her trying

To figure out,
for this small soul,
some way to keep her parenthood whole.

Now that
the decision's made…
grandmother, yes-but-not… life stayed

The same, but fundamental change
occurred. My response… to cry… is not so strange.

I am bereft.

    I mentioned, before, that I expected me to be more rational, more reasonable than I expected others to be. I felt so bad at this point, I had to find out why. This was why… I was grieving, as I had been for most of the past seven or eight months. I grieved my innocent daughter; I grieved my lost successful mother image; I grieved the normalcy of family life for my other children as well as for myself; this list goes on and on. Now, I grieved my little first grandchild. (I wonder if she'll ever believe that. Certainly, she'll look back and know that at some point, we "gave her up." Well, not without a fight, and certainly, only after we'd made sure she would have a happy home.)

I must mention that Steph made one last attempt to keep Karynna with her. She called from school and cried and told me there must be a way for her to parent the baby and still go to school. I told her to call her counselor, call her advisor at school, talk to the people who know the way the charitable programs work; to pull out all the stops. I told her that she needed to assure herself she was doing the best thing possible for Karynna if she was to live with it. She did, though to what degree I don't know. I just know that a few days later, she had made her peace with her decision and promised Pat and Jeff that if they took the baby home, she wouldn't come after her during the three months she legally had to change her mind. Thoughtful, even in grief. Now, she would depend on their communications and the pictures they would send — small consolation.

My child, do not forget my teaching,
but let your heart keep my commandments;
for length of days and years of life
and abundant welfare they will give you.
Do not let loyalty and faithfulness forsake you;
bind them around your neck,
write them on the tablet of your heart.
So you will find favor and good repute
in the sight of God and of people.
Trust in the Lord with all your heart,
and do not rely on your own insight.
In all your ways acknowledge him,
and he will make straight your paths.
Do not be wise in your own eyes;
fear the Lord, and turn away from evil.
It will be a healing for your flesh
and a refreshment for your body.
Honor the Lord with your substance
and with the first fruits of all your produce;
then your barns will be filled with plenty,
and your vats will be bursting with wine.
My child, do not despise the Lord's discipline
or be weary of his reproof,
for the Lord reproves the one he loves,
as a father the son in whom he delights.

PROVERBS 3:1-12

Letter and Birthday Card to Stephanie

Dear Steph,

Here we are, just a few days before your 20th birthday. I hope it'll be a year of progress and happiness.

What I expect it to be is a difficult year, from time to time, whenever you think about Karynna, but also a hopeful year when you think about her. I hope you'll remember to pray for her and her new family, daily. Infancy is such a dangerous time of life. As for me, I pray for you all AND for our family. I showed Aunt Kathy, Susie, Bernice, cousin Chris and Grandma Colwell the pictures of Karynna on Sunday at the picnic. Grandma says she looks just like you did as a baby.

Meanwhile, you'll be getting your energy back pretty soon, and you'll have to channel it into positive directions. Don't let Karynna down. She's going to grow up knowing you were in college at the time she was born. Show her what a lot of positive energy can lead to. You're halfway there. Don't let anymore detours sway you from your course. What's your goal? Get to it, and don't let any college distractions keep you from it from here on in, okay? I wish you the best.

Good Luck!

Love,
Mom

This was the letter I sent in the card I made and mentioned earlier. By now, my fears for her future decisions had come to a head. I tried to make my letter supportive and helpful. I don't know how she saw it... probably meddling and irritating. I prayed that the message Stephanie *needed* to get was what she *would* get from this letter.

We have this hope, a sure and steadfast anchor
of the soul, a hope that enters the inner shrine
behind the curtain, where Jesus,
a forerunner on our behalf, has entered,
having become a high priest forever
according to the order of Melchizedek.

HEBREWS 6:19-20

Adoptive Mother Pat's Letter to Stephanie, Just Before Steph's Birthday

Dear Stephanie,

I sit and write this letter in such joy but also with my heart aching for you and what you are going through. Steph, I know how it feels to let go of a child and I promise you your daughter and mine will always know that you made a decision that was the hardest thing for you because you loved her so much. She will grow up knowing she has 2 mothers that love her. This has been a long difficult process for you, but we have been so impressed with your strength and honesty. I will try and raise your daughter with those same traits.

Jeff and I promise to always love this baby. We will provide everything so that she can grow to be the strong, healthy, loving woman that you are. I appreciate having you tell Carol about your promise to me and remember I promise to always share with you the pictures and letters so you will know how special she is.

Take care of yourself and know that we will give her all the love and care she needs and deserves.

Your daughter and mine will always be special because we were able to come together to do what is best for her. I truly believe God brought us together so we could both love this little girl. She will be surrounded by people who love her so she can grow to be a secure and happy woman. I promise you I will do everything possible to keep her safe, healthy and happy because you have already done so much for her.

God Bless You!

Love,
Pat

Pleasant speech multiplies friends,
and a gracious tongue multiplies courtesies.
Let those who are friendly with you be many,
but let your advisers be one in a thousand.
When you gain friends, gain them through testing,
and do not trust them hastily.
For there are friends who are such when it suits them,
but they will not stand by you in time of trouble.
And there are friends who change into enemies,
and tell of the quarrel to your disgrace.
And there are friends who sit at your table,
but they will not stand by you in time of trouble.
When you are prosperous, they become your second self,
and lord it over your servants;
but if you are brought low, they turn against you,
and hide themselves from you.
Keep away from your enemies,
and be on guard with your friends.
Faithful friends are a sturdy shelter:
whoever finds one has found a treasure.
Faithful friends are beyond price;
no amount can balance their worth.
Faithful friends are life-saving medicine;
and those who fear the Lord will find them.
Those who fear the Lord direct their friendship aright,
for as they are, so are their neighbors also.

SIRACH 6:5-17

Letter to Charmain

Dear Charmain,

I've been thinking, since 8/26, of writing to you to let you
know how it goes with us, and I've finally gotten around to it.

August 26, one day before the birthday of my sister, Stephanie's Godmother, Stephanie's baby was born. She named her Karynna Joan (without knowing, I think, that Joan was a favorite name of my Mother's), I got a phone call from Stephanie, today (she's been back to school since August 22!), and understand the adoptive family has renamed her... Peyton Stephanie. The baby was 4 lb. 13 1/2 oz., 18 in., and had a lot of dark hair, just as Stephanie did when she was born. My mother thinks she looks (she saw photos; she didn't go to visit) just like Stephanie as a baby.

We had some rough times before the birth... premature labor about a week before, which was stopped with medication. Then, in the space of five days (it probably would have been three days, but there was a weekend in the middle, and everything stops for that!), she had three sonograms, at three different locations! They all agreed that the baby was suffering intrauterine growth retardation, and couldn't pinpoint just why. Everyone was always asking about smoking, which Stephanie insisted she had stopped as soon as she found she was pregnant. So, strangely, they decided to induce labor, because the baby would probably grow better outside the womb. The high-risk center at Allegheny General got us, once again... Dr. Denver, at Sewickley, didn't want to take any unnecessary risks... so we were dealing with the same Dr. Thomas that we had met earlier, when they thought Steph might have had gestational diabetes. He said the baby might actually lose weight in these last weeks, instead of gaining. Well, I don't know if I agree, but we have to hope they know their jobs.

Karynna/Peyton had trouble eating and keeping it down and, therefore, in gaining weight for a week or so. She went home after a week and a half, with monitors. I never really knew her physical condition. No one apparently felt I would be interested. Although I visited a few times while she was hos-

pitalized, all I knew I gleaned from Stephanie, and from looking around while I was there. The rules even forbade grandparents from visiting with the baby if a parent was not there!

Things settled down, once the baby went home. Up until
then, Steph (not to mention everyone else) was tormented by
the thought that she should find some way to "keep her." I
racked my brain (such as it is) over and over again, trying to
figure out something, anything, that would be better than never
seeing this child again, and I couldn't come up with it. Something, I suspect, that that child will never understand. Unfortunately, with these less-than-ideal circumstances, we knew all
the choices stunk. That's how I felt. The hugest weight I felt was
that I had to choose how to support Stephanie, based on what
I knew of her needs. She, of course, is not aware of her imma-
turity. We were quite certain that parenthood, at this time,
would be a great adventure… for about two weeks. Giving her
the benefit of the doubt, then maybe for a few months. She had
some friends offering to baby-sit; she'd heard she could go on
Welfare and use one of the daycare-like charitable organiza-
tions while she was at class. We'd said we'd baby-sit like normal grandparents, a couple of times a month, etc. Finally, after
a late-evening session of worrying over the phone (that
Karynna would never forgive her, that she was not doing the
right thing with planning adoption, that we had such a large
family, she just couldn't believe no one would "come through"
for her, though she never asked anyone to take the baby, etc.),
I suggested she try all roads… make sure she left no stone
unturned, because she'd feel guilty about it later… check with
the school social-worker, call her counselor, etc. She did, and
by the next day, she'd realistically decided that she was not
ready to be a parent. The nurses at the hospital told her the baby
would require very careful watching for awhile, and she knew
she couldn't do that and stay in school. She can see that school

is the only way she'll ever get that independence she desires so strongly. A different daughter, different circumstances, and we might have had a little person here, making me so busy that I wouldn't have time for this letter.

Sadly, we knew that Stephanie and we can't coexist peacefully in the same household. This is my biggest regret. My Mother told me of a second-cousin who became pregnant at 16. Her mother told her that she and the baby could live with them, but the child and childcare were all hers. When it became possible, the cousin got her GED, and then I don't know if she went to college or not. This, I know, is what my Mother probably hoped for us. It is as much an admission of my inability to handle my daughter as it is a statement about her behavior, that we could not do things this way.

I also got some family feedback that consisted of wondering if sending her back to the same environment (La Roche College) was such a good idea. We had given her the option of transferring to another school, and starting over, but it did not suit her. She did not feel the embarrassment we felt, and she needed the support of her friends. I only hope they are… her friends. Sometimes, I guess you might guess, I wonder.

Well, now, we all have to live with the decision that's been made. We know the adoptive parents, Pat and Jeff, are happy. She sent Stephanie a note that was very gracious, caring and precious. I hope she never forgets that that is all we have to hang onto: pictures and letters. Steph, for her part, has promised not to show up at the end of the three months she has to make up her mind, and claim the baby as hers again. Thankfully, she's thinking of Karynna. What a wrench that would be for a little child and those she's become accustomed to as her parents.

Meanwhile, we all go through the process of grieving for this little girl. My Mother-in-law actually visited the baby in the hospital. Both she and my Mother have cried and cried about this. It was heartbreaking telling them when she was born. I felt so cheated out of being elated and blabbing the news to everyone. I called them and my sister, Kathy, who asked me to let her know when it happened. I couldn't do any more.

Well, I've got two of the baby's pictures in my wallet, just in case anyone wants to see them. Several friends have actually looked at the whole couple of rolls of pictures of this tiny little face. I have some true friends.

My sister, Susan, for her part, felt it necessary to include a note in her birthday card to her Goddaughter, Stephanie. It made Steph so mad she was breathing fire when she called to tell me about it. My sister covered a whole world of information, starting each sentence with an "I'm sorry you...." I hope to get hold of it, so I can make a copy. Stephanie complained that it was all stuff she already knew, and why did Aunt Susie want to make her so miserable when she already felt so bad? Well, that part bothered me, but I mentioned that maybe she didn't want to wait too long to get it all said, because people had been known to make this same mistake more than once! I hope that she will someday come to appreciate Aunt Susie's concern, since it was such that she didn't care what Stephanie's opinion of her would be, as long as she got the information she should get from her Godmother. Right now, Aunt Susie will be lucky if she gets a thank you card for the money she sent!

Well, we're surviving. My husband just celebrated his 51st birthday, and we have what look like normal days. I even feel almost ordinary, until someone asks me how I am. My answer hasn't been "Fine," since this started in January. I'm still just "Hanging in there," and "Doin' okay." I feel foolish when I think about how much worse life could be. I feel terrified when I think what might still be in store for us. Mostly, though, I just realize this was our torture for the present, and there is a possibility that some good growing might have happened this year. In all of us. And I sure hope so.

Thanks for being there for me. I've needed and appreciated you more than you probably know. Thanks.

Love,
Donna

P.S. I don't know what the problem was, but I never got this lengthy letter out of the computer and into the mail. Sorry it's so late. We're doing better. My daughter called from school, today, and said she got her first set of photographs of Peyton and family, and she got another letter from Pat, which she read over the phone. Boy, are *they* happy. The baby grew to 5 lb. 4 oz. by her second week checkup, and they think she looks great in pink. I hope I get to see these pictures before they're old news. Steph doesn't care to spend too much time here. I wonder if I'd be able to ask Pat to keep me informed, or if that's overstepping the bounds, here. Do you get to see pictures and receive a letter now and again?

My brothers and sisters,
whenever you face trials of any kind,
consider it nothing but joy,
because you know that the testing
of your faith produces endurance;
and let endurance have its full effect,
so that you may be mature
and complete, lacking in nothing.

JAMES 1:2-4

Survivors

We're here, we've made it;
another hurricane along the way,
met and weathered.

We're both starting to look as if
we've had sunburns and near-drownings,
unmeasured.

Hail! John Francis Paul,
captain of a sea-tested, storm-tried
frigate named Rosser...
May the long, deep ocean, ahead,
be temperate, and your only tempests be
in teacup and saucer.

Believe it or not, this verse was my birthday card for my
husband, John. It was nearly a month since Karynna Joan/
Peyton Stephanie was born. Life's frantic routine was in full
swing, and I could go a while, now and again, without think-

94

ing about her. I was still concerned about Stephanie. I suspected she was no longer going to church, which she had continued to do all during the summer, although she did not attend the same Mass as did we. Different friends would, from time to time, tell me they'd seen her at the 12 o'clock service. Now that she was back at school, she was not coming home, and I had the feeling she was angry with God. Since this could lead to enormous problems we hadn't dealt with yet, I was still praying and lighting votive candles constantly.

That reminds me of an occasion, years ago, when I was speaking to the mother of one of Stephanie's classmates. She told me of her son who had "made her crazy." He did all the rebellious hair and clothing stuff that drives parents mad, and appeared to be heading down the wrong path. She said she had told him he was making her into a saint! I laughed heartily when she said that, and she looked straight at me and said, "I'm not joking." She wasn't. He had sent her straight to God, and I'd begun to understand that fully, once Stephanie had begun her "trial of the parents."

Steph was making me into a saint, too. I don't know how successfully. One thing was for sure… daily Mass, which I'd begun once Jeff and Greg were in Kindergarten, was a lifesaver. Morning prayers, Scripture reading, and a fifteen-decade Rosary each day kept me afloat.

All I can say, along with the real saints,
is PRAY! Pray always! I'm not joking.
My pampered children have traveled rough roads;
they were taken away like a flock carried off by the enemy.
Take courage, my children, and cry to God,
for you will be remembered by
the one who brought this upon you.
For just as you were disposed to go astray from God,
return with tenfold zeal to seek him.
For the one who brought these calamities upon you
will bring you everlasting joy with your salvation.

BARUCH 4:26-29

Coping

Just knowing you were sadder-than-sad can make me blue.
And hoping you are coping (That's all to ask of you.),

Compels me, now, to send you a card to let you see
What happens to you, and how you feel, both mean a lot to me.

Keeping busy's important, but that's not all there is;
Make sure that you are rested, to do well on test and quiz,

But, finally, when your heart is tired of aching and stumbling
      around,
You might want to search out the chapel — upon God's ear
      to pound.

He's heard it all before. He can handle your distress.
He can take your bluest day and hear your "worst confess,"

Then, somehow, when it's over; when you look back upon it all,
You'll see that He has answered — every single time you'd call.

A note with this poem states, "For Stephanie, after phone call." I have an undulating kind of "phonophobia" (I named this myself), and I was getting very anxious about answering the phone. Talking to Stephanie was difficult. Probably the way my friends felt when they had to deal with me for the past 10 months! All I could do was offer support and pray she would go the right way. She was losing weight like mad, and although plunged into an agony of grief, it was still necessary that she maintain a decent average at school. (Aside from the need to look valuable to an employer eventually, she had to hang onto her "Dean's Award" of $3,000.00 a year in tuition, now.) No doubt about it, she had made her life very hard. As usual, harder than it had to be. Finally, I'd run out of anger about it. I could only feel sorry that she seemed destined to complicate her life. And life's already complicated enough.

Praise the Lord!
I will give thanks to the Lord
with my whole heart,
in the company of the upright,
in the congregation.
Great are the works of the Lord,
studied by all who delight in them.
Full of honor and majesty is his work,
and his righteousness endures forever.

PSALM 111:1-3

The Sun Still Shines

The sky's still where it ought to be
    though it may be gray and stormy.
The sun still shines — above it all —
    though there be rain before me.

As weather comes and weather goes, so
    emotional seas may rage,
But through it all, we recognize
    the kind of battle we wage,

And set our sights on what is right;
    on doing our best; on good,
And once in a while, we look up to see
    the sky… as blue as it could
                ever be!

After Spring break, Steph called home one day, and sounded quite sad on the phone. I just hoped to offer some support of the "hang in there" kind. Surely, she must have times of great distress, when she thinks about the little girl that she might have been raising. As for me, I've had a couple of experiences where someone was exuberantly telling me of the blessings of grandchildren, believing I hadn't any as yet. Some, I let talk and simply agreed that it's wonderful for them to so enjoy it. Another one or two, I have let in on my little secret, and to watch their faces fall so swiftly is enough to keep me from mentioning it to anyone for a very long time. That doesn't mean they handled my information incorrectly, just that they know the joy of a grandchild they can hold and love, and they feel sorry for us. At least our grandchild is still getting held and hugged. Just not by us.

I'd begun to feel such a desire to have little Peyton know us, that I even discussed it with my Mom (who, by the way, told me how difficult it was to be unable to share her great-grandchild with those who whipped out the pictures at a moment's notice). At her suggestion, I began keeping a journal of letters to Peyton in a blank book my Mother gave me years ago. Someday, maybe she'll want to know about us, and even if I'm not around anymore, she'll know some of what I thought. I do hope that she'll want it, someday. I so very much want her to have it.

Working Up To One

You've worked your way to this fine day,
    and we know it was a job.
Finally, we meet you here,
    about to turn the knob

On one year old! It's magical!
    We're glad that it's okay
For us to send a present;
    to wish you a happy day.

You've so many wonderful triumphs;
    a whole year's worth to show.
We think you're looking pretty good,
    and wanted you to know.
                Atta girl!

Our first grandchild made it to one year old. As a mother,
I was always so worried about crib deaths, and the illnesses

little babies get. It is a real accomplishment to make it to age one, and frequently it means a lot less to worry about. I found out that Peyton had spent 5 1/2 months wearing a monitor. I am so glad I didn't know that. She also had some kind of intestinal problem that led her to throw up her feedings (much like Stephanie had), for months. Yes, she really is doing much better, now. She's starting to look happier in her photos. More smiles are showing up.

Stephanie and I went shopping, together, for gifts for Peyton's first birthday. Shopping is not something I do very willingly, or often, so this was remarkable. We both bought her little outfits for Fall/Winter. I hope her parents think of taking a picture of her in them and sending them our ways. I'd really like to see her in them.

This card is the first correspondence I actually sent. All the rest is slowly accumulating in that less-than-blank book in which I began writing to Peyton, in January... three days before I turned 45 years old; one year after I was "forced onto a new road when our unmarried daughter got pregnant."

But Moses said to the Lord, "If you please, Lord,
I have never been eloquent,
neither in the past nor recently, nor even
now that you have spoken to your servant;
but I am slow of speech and slow of tongue."
Then the Lord said to him,
"Who gives one man speech,
and makes another deaf and dumb?
Is it not I, the Lord? Go, then!
It is I who will assist you in speaking
and will teach you what you are to say."

EXODUS 4:10-12

Life at God's Seat

Knowing the purpose;
    following through;
Taking each minute
    and making it do
Whatever chore it's been
    given to hold;
Feeling the feeling
    through which it's been rolled
Persevering
    through both good and bad;
Choosing the classic
    beneath the fad…
This is our job;
    our challenge to meet,
Leading, finally,
    to great joy at God's seat.

Believe it or not, this was my first attempt this year at a Christmas card verse! I'm fairly certain it's not going to be the one I use, but I sure thought it fit this book. We just keep trudging, trying, plugging along... trying to discern God's purpose in all that comes our way and accepting this imperfect life for what it is. It's not meant to be all fun and games here. Life is also a trial. So, when the good (and there are many small but wonderful goods in each and every day) comes along, we must look up and be grateful... we did not deserve it, but God sent it, anyway. Isn't that great!

He was praying in a certain place, and after he had finished,
one of his disciples said to him, "Lord, teach us to pray,
as John taught his disciples." He said to them,
"When you pray, say:

Father, hallowed be your name.
Your kingdom come.
Give us each day our daily bread.
And forgive us our sins,
for we ourselves forgive
everyone in debt to us,
And do not bring us to the time of trial."

Luke 11:1-4

ST PAULS

This book was designed and published by St. Pauls/ Alba House, the publishing arm of the Society of St. Paul, an international religious congregation of priests and brothers dedicated to serving the Church through the communications media. For information regarding this and associated ministries of the Pauline Family of Congregations, write to the Vocation Director, Society of St. Paul, 7050 Pinehurst, Dearborn, Michigan 48126. Phone (313) 582-3798 or check our internet site, www.albahouse.org